THE TAO OF TARO
TARO ZION JOY

Love is sent

◆ FriesenPress

One Printers Way
Altona, MB R0G 0B0
Canada

www.friesenpress.com

Copyright © 2022 by Taro Zion Joy
First Edition — 2022

All rights reserved.

Foreword by Penelope Joy and Alexander Arbess-Joy

Cover painting by Miles Lowry "One Wave For The Storm Moon" 2021 mileslowry.ca

All rights reserved. No part of this book may be reproduced or used in any manner without written permission of the copyright owner except for the use of quotations in a book review. For more information, address: djalexjoy@gmail.com.

www.thetaooftaro.com

No part of this publication may be reproduced in any form, or by any means, electronic or mechanical, including photocopying, recording, or any information browsing, storage, or retrieval system, without permission in writing from FriesenPress.

ISBN
978-1-03-914867-3 (Hardcover)
978-1-03-914866-6 (Paperback)
978-1-03-914868-0 (eBook)

1. BIOGRAPHY & AUTOBIOGRAPHY, PERSONAL MEMOIRS

Distributed to the trade by The Ingram Book Company

With love
Peggy
Penny,

THE TAO OF TARO

Love issuy

Foreword

by Alexander Arbess-Joy

It was, for all of us who loved him, not an easy love. It was a love that truly tested the meaning of love, and that is ultimately what I believe he was here for, to test what love meant.

It was my great honour to be the brother of Taro John Zion Joy. Our time was spent travelling the world, swimming with dragons, blasting down mountainsides, exploring uncharted places, rocking club after club, trekking through rainforests, climbing mountains, training in martial arts, loving, and generally making the most of life. It was tremendous! We served as each other's guardians—always a hand to grab onto at the edge of the precipice. Life was a constant adventure!

Taro's bright light cast a long shadow, which was part of his wild genius. He journeyed to the dark night of the soul many times, learning difficult lessons, which are shared in his writing. His passing leaves a hole in my heart through the fullness of the life we lived. His legacy lives on through his friends and family whom he loved without end. Here's to Taro! A rare and exceptional soul!! Continue to let love guide the way!!

Loveissent

Welcome to the Tao of Taro

Early Days
by Penelope Joy

He gave me his name in a dream. I am standing on a beach at water's edge, warm wind on my back, a wavelet rolls over my toes. I look down. A letter appears in the firm, wet sand, then another, each etched with a bamboo stick dragged by unseen hand. Slowly, carefully, four letters appear: T-A-R-O. I put my fingers down and trace the damp letters, tiny pools catch the sun's rays and reflect water.

Taro's first cradle was a plaited shopping basket blowing in the breeze off the limb of a frangipani tree on Little Jost Van Dyke, smallest of the British Virgin Islands. There he crawled in the sand after tiny scuttling crabs and laughed as a passing butterfly grazed his skin. Turning and rolling he gazed up at a swooping booby bird in the clear sky.

In Formentera in the Balearics, he learned to swim in the Mediterranean, laughing and splashing with our two puppies, Spotty and Muldoon, curling up to sleep under the beams of a four-hundred-year-old finca, waking and sleeping with the sun.

Later, in Canada, on the first day of pre-school, he climbed out of a bathroom window and set off down the road with his brand-new lunch kit. I got a concerned call from staff. He was located in a nearby park sharing his peanut butter snacks with a squirrel. I hurried over . . .

'What's the matter, hon? Didn't you like school? Wasn't it fun?'

'They . . . ' he sniffed, trying to hide his tears, 'they made us sit on **chairs**'!

Prospects for schooling did not seem good. It didn't improve. Later, reports started coming in: 'possibly dyslexic' . . . 'very disruptive in class . . . 'constantly late or absent' . . .

The smiling preschool teacher spoke to me with polite condescension.

'Taro is a little unsettled in the classroom. Of course, it would help if he could arrive on time in the morning . . .'

My face flushed. I never did do mornings well, and Taro was not going to do a thing to do with school unless seriously coerced. I rose awkwardly from the pint-sized chair I'd been obliged to perch on, and walked home from school through the back lane.

Our little wooden cabin on East 55th was more suited to a Gulf Island acreage than a Vancouver city street. Across the tiny yard lay a small renovated woodshed, Taro's room. That evening, I tried again to explain the value of his teacher, but he was having nothing of it.

'She just wants us to sit in lines and get excited about sticking macaroni on paper plates. . . .'

'I'm sure that's not all she does . . .'

'Yeah—you don't know, Mom . . .'

It went on and on, me trying to be reasonable and caring and 'a good mother', him getting more and more angry. Eventually I ordered him to bed, with all the mindless authoritarian demands that I so hated hearing from my own mother . . . he marched off across the yard to his little cabin room.

I sat trying to breathe through the turmoil in my brain. Frustration, anger, despair. Where was the magical child that I had birthed? The baby who told me his name in a dream, that I later learned had a Japanese Samurai connection. Where was I?

I washed the dishes, watched a bit of dreadful television, read the Arts Section of *The Globe and Mail*, and finally decide to go to bed. The clock read 12:30. I glanced out to the cabin to see the light still on in his room. I marched angrily across to the cabin. The little bugger, he'll still be playing with his race-track cars, and here it is 12:30; he'll never wake up in the morning and we'll be late again . . . Before opening the door, I glanced through the lighted window, and stopped. His crayons lay beside his hand in technicolour turmoil. He was hunched over doing something on a piece of paper with such intensity that an aura glowed around him. Clearer than if he'd been yelling through a megaphone, I heard the message:

'Back Off! Keep Out! Important Creative Work in Progress!'

I went quietly back to bed.

Next morning, a replay of innumerable dreary mornings: me half awake, cursing the alarm; he resentful at being roused, fighting against getting up, grouchy about eating breakfast, me searching blearily around to find material for his school lunch, both overlooked by the clock ticking relentlessly. He is finally out the door on the way to school—perhaps. I sit to drink a tepid cup of coffee. Warm bed beckons mightily but I force myself to resist and start clearing breakfast dishes. Then I remember the vision that I had seen through his window the previous night. I stumble over my slippers, cross again out to his cabin, open the door, and step up into his little room . . . and there it is. On his school desk (a battered artifact hauled home from a nearby garage sale), sits a big sheet of card carrying the image of an extraordinary bird—a drawing of such power and energy that it makes me step back. Vibrant, multi-hued feathers, coloured beak, and long tail—a quetzal-like bird takes flight from the page, transforming the drab surroundings with indescribable majesty. This steed of many colours seems poised to fly to the far reaches of the universe. This, I know, is his magic carpet, his vehicle of escape. Something very important has been created. Then I see the words—words written clearly, eloquently, with a firm flowing hand, words written by a boy who had never written a single letter coherently in class, words written in the middle of the night by a child who is being called dyslexic, incompetent, and is already sidelined into special ed. classes. The words make me smile, restore belief in the son that I know, the words read 'The Life Bird'. Letters follow the slope of the bird's back as if being blown by a breeze as it takes flight, an illustration so much a piece, so complete a force field of exuberance that I dare not touch it. I sit and gaze for a long time.

I knew then that this child had access to powers and resources that would guide and protect him through a life that would not be easy, but would never be ordinary.

Much later, he was to write:

> The bird . . . what is it with that bird? You always seemed so impressed with it, Mom, like there was some hope for me because I created it. As if by rendering that bird I proved that I was connected to something sacred, that made me greater than the sum of all the trouble I always caused. It was just a bird to me, something I drew . . . wasn't it? I know now I did not really draw The Life Bird; I know it flew through me. I had no idea what I was drawing that night, no thought of a bird as I moved every colour in the box across the page in passionate scribble. There was no bird there until that was what was on the page, and then, of course, I knew it was The Life Bird. Now, I can recognise that breakthrough moment, that link to the memory hotline. There is a moment for a child in the process of creation when a line is crossed from being the only person who can see the subject to being the creator of a subject that everyone can recognise. The Life Bird was that moment for me. I knew I must never forget how to be a child. You were right, Mom, the bird was relevant, a very important part of our history, one you recognised so long ago, one that today I finally understand. Years later, The Life Bird would return in my dreams. Aged and risen, Phoenix-like, it transported me through time and space—it was one of the first of my many stories.

Table of Contents

Foreword	v
Early Days	vi
The River	1
How Do I Love?	11
Invitation to Ecstasy	13
On Wealth	15
Just So	17
Midnight Mass	19
The Three-Minute Poem	22
The Nightlife	24
Paris November 2015	27
Baseball Bats to Vipassana	29
Constriction (Plant Prohibition)	31
White Knight	32
Hard Choice Fast	39
New Beginnings	45
Just Breathe	48
Transmission	49
Kannon	51
I Miss Tokyo	56
Come Home Now, Child	59
Fatherhood	62
I Want for my daughter	64
First Breath	66
The Door (for my mother)	70
With This Feather	72
When You Speak a Word to Someone	74
I Hear the Universe in You	75
Burning Down Libraries	78
A Perfect Storm	80
Four Truths of a First Burn	81
Polish Your Joy	93
Dying	95
Eternum	97
Finale	99
From Brother to Brother	101
About the Book	104
Acknowledgements	105
About the Author	106

The River

Some stories remain fresh forever; they are in the flesh, flow in the blood, and bind to the soul as tight as woven steel. This is not a story of courage nor one of stupidity (no matter how you measure it); it is a story of wanting to be greater, to grow and move in ways that most can only dream. It is about a turning point on a razor's edge in a mighty storm; it is about stacking the odds far against oneself to try and prove the existence of a god. It is not mine alone. It belongs to Justin, Rain, Coal, and the Thompson River, main tributary to the Fraser, precursor to the famous Hell's Gate.

That year, we had taken a few trips to raft its famous rapids; we had a friend who knew a guy running a rafting outfit that led trips down 18 rapids along its twisting body. Class 3, 4, and 5 rapids will do everything from entertain to scare the shit out of you, as eight-man crews, with one rafting master, paddle their way through some of the most beautiful and heaviest rapids in Canada. Those trips were great but, at our age and with our high capacity for adrenalin, we were not entirely satisfied with the action. We (meaning mostly me) took to jumping out of the boat at particularly hairy points in the rapids to "freestyle" them. To this we added some LSD, perhaps mixed with mescaline, and found that the "action" improved significantly. With our thick life preservers firmly attached, we had only to remember, as much as possible, to keep our heads above water and our feet pointed downriver to avoid having our skulls cracked on any of the many rocks that pepper segments of the river. This antic was fun, made the boat master none too happy, but eventually lost its 'rush'.

Around that time, it came to me, "The Prayer to the River". Part poem, part prayer, part prophecy, it was an homage to the

Thompson's mighty power, and a call to the spirits of whatever gods may or may not exist there, to protect my brothers and myself as we entered a challenge that would surely be a life-changing experience. It contained an acceptance that the day would be unlike any other and that, should we be allowed to sit together at its end, it would be unlike anywhere we had ever been before.

I remember the drive up in Rain's blue Mustang GT, with a white racing stripe down the centre. Stereo blasting Rage Against the Machine.

> *"Fuck you, I won't do what you tell me!! Fuck you, I won't do what you tell me!! Fuck you, I won't do what you tell me!!"*

Those three repeated lines summed it up for our generation and hit particularly close to home for the four of us. We stopped a couple times to sit with hundreds of other tourists watching the rapids move thousands of tonnes of water at breakneck speed between high stone cliffs and 200-tonne boulders. We listened to the raft crews screaming as they plunged headlong into the mist. Bubbles boiled on the surface of an underwater current that, in one spot and time in history, had held a train car and eight people aboard, spinning inside it for a week.

We sat in silence imagining our route, kinaesthetically training for the swim we were about to make, repeating our mantra from Frank Herbert's novel *Dune*:

> *"Fear is the mind killer"*.

We could do this—all of us fit, with ample water experience (except Justin, who was thus perhaps the most courageous, or dumbest, of us all). Rain was, in effect, a type of fish, having been a swim instructor, with as powerful an arsenal of swim strokes as any I have seen. Coal, who looked every bit the name he had chosen, appeared, in the right light, carved out of that compound. He enjoyed surfing the freezing Canadian waves whenever he got a chance. Then there was me, at my peak in fitness, martially trained, limber from years of dance, and deep into the idea that the mind could overcome whatever it encountered.

In the trunk of the GT, we all had wetsuits, five-point-five millimetre, with hoods, and seven-millimetre booties and gloves. More than enough to bring you to the surface after a crashing fall off a huge wave in the salt-saturated oceans of BC. We had spent days in the ocean, during snowfall in the winter, walking out at sunset, steaming from exertion. We were convinced that we would have the necessary buoyancy to stay afloat and the insulation to stay warm for at least five hours in the much warmer river water.

We drove and drove until there were no more tourist stops and no more river tour outlets and no more houses of any consequence. We found a dirt road that led to a little used entrance to, at that point, the river's calm waters. We came to the end of the road (metaphor not lost here) and discovered, adjacent to what seemed to be public access to the river, a small farmhouse. After a few minutes of standing around staring at the water that whisked hypnotically by, we were approached by a kindly looking old man. He asked our intention and we told him we had come to swim the Thompson. He had a laugh about crazy kids but said it was done all the time and asked if we would like to borrow some life vests that he would happily lend us. We explained that the buoyancy of our wetsuits would be fine and how we wanted to move with the water, not bob like fishing lures down its body. He laughed, wished us luck, and went on his way. Bolstered by the knowledge that this had been done before and encouraged by the lightness of this old man's observations, we suited up in preparation.

Before we entered the water, we gathered together. We had the poem/prayer, and each one of us committed some part of ourselves to this journey; we all absolved each other from what was about to happen, should it go bad for one of us. We then took communion, which, in this case, was a high dose of LSD, mixed with a concoction a chemist friend of ours had come up with called "Fusion".

Years later, while watching an anti-drug show, I noticed that Fusion had a lot of the nicer-sounding side effects of PCP. We received our holy flesh as such, and drank the blood, which, in this instance, was a good chug of Wild Turkey. We entered the water.

The first couple of hours were great, the water pristine; as our minds expanded, so did its beauty. Here, the river was wide, shore mostly rocky beach or farmland, punctuated by the occasional house or river tour operation. When passing these, we would go low in the water, black hoods up on our wetsuits. We believed we would have appeared as four silent buoys floating past, or lost jetsam from some overturned canoe or, at worst, garbage illegally dumped upriver by some moron. We did this partially to conceal our journey and partially because we were far too high to try and explain ourselves to anyone.

At this point along the river, the class 2 and 3 rapids were as fun as any water we had ever swum. Rough currents in relatively shallow water spat us airborne, if we paddled at the right speed and angle. We were becoming masters of the water, learning to chase lines through rapids that would give back to us the greatest value for effort. On the few occasions when rafts passed by on their way to the big stuff, we would bark like seals and fling ourselves off the top of some small rapid wave near to the boat. I can only imagine what the people in those boats thought. River seals are a rare sight in the Thompson!

A few hours into the trip, we arrived at the first class 5 rapid along the journey known as "The Frog" for the house-size rock that split this mighty river down the centre and sent waterfalls off either side a good forty feet down to the mayhem below. Having pretty much breezed through class 4 and enjoyed it as a dolphin might enjoy riding the wake of a large ferry, we figured that the big boys couldn't be much worse. We first heard it far off in the distance, a rumbling that caused the surface of the flat (and now very deep) water to permanently ripple, then we felt the increased speed of water flow and watched as the flat edges of the river grew upwards into unclimbable walls of rock. We huddled together, arms linked, tried to control our breathing and heart rates and hyper oxygenate ourselves for what was obviously going to be a rough ride. We were all hallucinating, but no amount of psychedelics could overwhelm the vast majesty of nature at its full screaming pinnacle of violence. This was water fighting rock for control of eternity.

Then came the clouds. Not clouds sent from heaven to block the sun on this crystal-clear day, but a tiny weather pattern created solely by the violence and volume of the water that was churning ahead of us. We saw tourists at the top of lookouts pointing at us and training their cameras on us as we moved inescapably towards the beast before us. We clung tight to each other and reminded one another that the boats broke for the right side of The Frog, telling us that the left had too many boulders below it. We told each other we loved one another and tried to comfort each other as our speed picked up and the noise grew so loud that speech was impossible. We then broke apart and began to swim towards the right side of this giant stone that had glass-smooth waterfalls descending off each side into God only knew what form of vicious screaming nightmares that we were hearing from below. We tried to swim lightly, but to imagine we were swimming at all would imply we had some form of control over our trajectory, which was really like trying to skydive upwards against the awesome pull of gravity.

As I remember it, Justin was the first to go over. His scream sticks forever in my memory. "Oh god—No!!!" or something to that effect, was what I heard. The fact that I heard it from metres away when only moments before we could not shout loud enough into one another's ears to hear a word, bears testament to the volume and weight of his fear. Rain and Coal went silently into oblivion, and I, somewhere in-between, went about the business of meeting god on my own. I will never forget the sensation of pouring over a cliff with tonnes of water on my back and shooting first through the surface of the chaos below and then deep, deep below all that screaming mayhem. It was silent, peaceful as it grew steadily darker. Once, my peace was interrupted by impact with some unseen boulder, merely a brief distraction as I went about the process of dying. It is said that drowning, after the initial violence, is quite a peaceful way to die. To this I can testify. At first, of course, there was the fear and regret of going before my time, but then, as lungs began to fill, in-utero memories of breathing liquid. The brain starts to shut down its panic response; a beautiful peace comes over the soul, with quick acceptance that one's final moments have come. The light I was moving towards seemed predictable yet sanctified. Then, the sound of a million angels clapping at my arrival, brought me back from my perfect ascent to heaven. I was spat from the womb of this godlike river and quickly realised that the light was the surface and the clapping was the sound of rapids tearing deep wounds in any notion of peace around me. I was alive, a kilometre or so down the river, having travelled this distance deep under water out of sight of even the light of day, still in the frothing liquid centre of this madness, now alone and searching for my friends. In my heart, I believed they must be dead. I pulled left and right, with all my strength, in an attempt to imitate swimming where no swimming was possible.

From thirty yards off I saw him, moving like a great fish charging amongst the rapids; it was more a lunge from one freestanding wave to the next than a swim technique. Rain was piercing this river, over and over, as he filled the distance between us. I was paralyzed, transfixed, and barely aware of what mortal danger we were all in. Rain's ability to manoeuvre inside this cauldron was beyond conceiving; his grace testament to his martial commitment and physical ability. He reached me in seconds; looking into my terrified eyes, he grabbed my head with both hands and shouted, '*Not you Taro, not now, not you*'. This was all the time we had before chaotic torrents tore us apart, but it was the trigger that brought me back from the frozen end of fear and reminded me that I was still living and still had fight in me. I was allowed again to try and save my own life. For a second, I was swimming.

All of a sudden, falling as if in thin air, floating for a second on the edge of a vortex before descending into pure air, elemental and breathable, and merely a prelude to the murderous engine awaiting me at the bottom, I got caught in a whirlpool. Vague memories of an eight-man boat, with the whole crew fighting to get out of one of these pools, flashed across my mind as I was sucked into the hole in the water, churned around and spat back to the surface for the third time. It was to be my last. I felt strength sap from my limbs as water again filled my lungs; there was no fighting out of this beast, only violence followed by infinity. As I had these thoughts, I remember an orange pouch, followed by trailing blue, flying down the hole beside me. I reached out for it, if only because it was foreign, solid, and tangible in a world that would melt around fingers if you tried to hang onto it. A memory of river guides showing us how to use safety ropes flashed into disjointed, half-dead areas deep in my brain. Some unseen boat above the water was pulling me. Again, I lived. Every ounce of strength left in me focused as adrenalin centres fired, secretions I thought all but gone, ripped out of glands and fed pure fire into burnt-out muscles. I reached the boat and pulled myself into it, puking again and again till my lungs gave up their aquatic dividends and once again took air. Then a reconnoitre. I look around the staring wide eyes of Sunday tourists on a thrill ride who had just pulled a puking body from a screaming whirlpool, an incident which had, I imagine, put their particular boat in some danger. A hand on my back, boat guide asking me where the hell I came from and why didn't I have a life jacket on?

'*My friends, my friends, where are my friends?*' was my answer to any and all questions as we cruised out of the danger zone and approached, compared to where I had just been, peaceful waters. I stood, thanked the guide for saving me and said,

'*I cannot come home without them*' then stepped out of the boat into the turbulent melee that had just denied my death. I would search and find my friends or die with them. It had been my idea to do this and to live with their loss was no choice at all. I remember stepping out of the boat like I was stepping off a curb. I disappeared from the boat's view within seconds.

There was more of the same as I passed from rising wave to whirlpool like so much flotsam moving on the tide. I learned to pull against the water only when I needed to get results. I learned to breathe deeply when there was air and vomit underwater so as not to miss any chance to breathe. It became organic to move like this, to stay just on the edge of drowned and yet still be alive. Euphoria may not be quite the best description but it was akin; I became aware that for all its violence, it was beautiful in the sad way that dying must be. Then I saw him, up on the cliff ahead, perched like a falcon, hand held visor-like over eyes. Rain had made it to shore and was searching for us. Seeing me, he waved, and I swam again with a strength that was beyond any conscious knowledge of how exhausted I was. There was a rock dividing the rapid, on the far side of the river (from a highway looming somewhere above); there was a tiny beach carved amongst two-hundred-foot cliff walls of sheer stone. I swam with all my life, and, having once made shore, I looked back to see Coal, spread like crucified Christ on the back side of a rock in the centre of the river, Justin, sprawled on the narrow strip of sand, choking the last vestiges of water from his lungs. I had found them! We were alive, soon together, sitting on the far side of hell trying to figure out how we could possibly get out of this river anywhere within the next few miles. The rapid that sat before us was called the Jaws of Death. This was the spot that held down that train car and seven drowned men for a week before they could get to whatever was left of their bodies.

Across from our little sanctuary, separated by what looked like a series of bus-sized whirlpools, was an area of broken cliff and rocks tumbling into the river.

The rocks could be climbed to the highway far above. We were all hurt and beyond our capacities, but Justin was nearing critical condition and, though I have never articulated this, I will always remember that it was he who jumped first, untrained and out of shape, headfirst into this river, and survived. He was the strongest amongst us that day. It was decided we needed to get him out fast.

Mapping our route across an impossible, ever-changing liquid terrain, we (after seriously gathering as much strength as we could muster) re-entered the river and worked as a team to get Justin, and ourselves, to the other side as fast as possible. We operated on the strength of our love for each other, our happiness to all be together again, and our knowledge that our dear brother Justin could not survive this riverine trip any further. How we got across is a blur, but we did. We got Justin onto the rocks, and I gave him the car keys. He now had to climb a huge rocky cliff in a wetsuit, in the noonday sun, find the highway, hitch a ride back to the car, and meet us at river's end, where there was a parking lot adjacent to the water. Justin was six foot five, bald, heavyset, bordering on massive, covered in tattoos, and half dead. He had no easy task before him.

We continued down the river imagining that we had been through the worst and could swim our way to the final spot and survive the last two rapids that were not as large as what we had already survived. There were a few moments of peaceful floating, then some hairy areas where we were again fighting to breathe to stay above water. Then we saw what we knew was our end. It looked as if there was a highway of whirlpools stretched out across miles of glass-smooth water. Deep, impossible holes, spiralling in opposing directions, punctuated fast-moving but serenely flat water. It would be an impossible task; passing each whirlpool is like swimming against a rip tide. Once one is conquered, you are almost immediately fighting to clear another. We had passed three or four to get Justin out—I had nearly died in one; now we looked at possibly hundreds of them stretched before us. Here, the shore was accessible; it was time for us to begin our climb up its steep cliff face. We had been in the water six hours at this point, were shaking with the stress our bodies and souls had suffered but were happy as we struggled out of the river, peeled off the top half of our suits and allowed the sun to dry and heat our soaked bodies. The climb was brutal; along the way, we passed the train tracks that tipped that car full of bodies to their death so many years before. We prayed at so many spots that day, to so many gods for so many things; most of all we prayed to that mighty river, for sparing our lives, for showing us the majesty of her strength and, in a few brief hours, changing us all for life.

On the highway, we managed to get a ride with a very large, silent, Indian who merely asked if we came from the river. We told him we had. He motioned us to get in the back of his pickup, drove till we spotted Rain's car, where he pulled over.

We found Justin by the river, piling stones atop each other as markers for the friends he was sure he had lost that day. He was drinking whisky and crying out loud to the river, to God, to himself. Again, we were reunited, now, finally, we all allowed ourselves to cry. I still cry today when I remember how much love I saw in Justin's face as he worked his hands bloody, building memorials to us on the edge of the river. If you are ever lucky enough to have one friend like that, then God is great and you are blessed. I stood with three of them. That day will count, for all my years, as the moment when he smiled, and life was as good as it gets.

Photo: *Taro in a waterfall, Walbran Valley, British Columbia.*
Credit: Alexander Arbess-Joy.

How Do I Love?

I can't even find a word. What is love? What is this collection of letters that together seem to be reason enough for all acts—good, great, or horrific?
You deserve more than a single syllable.
You are more than a sound pushed through a throat and squeezed out of a mouth.
You and I are the eternal chant of shamans holding this fragile existence together.
You are every language to me, and more than that, you are none, nothing, silence in all its deafening magnitude.
You are the place in me before I ever spoke, when sound was an incantation,
Magic made by a goddess eventually known as 'Mother'.
I feel for you like the ocean does for rain.
You are the sky before it turned blue, the Earth before it knew it could grow jungles, feed civilization, bury treasure, power planets, and cure disease.
How did I come to this when I started speechless?
Hand to heart, head bowed.
If you never did another thing for me, I would already be in debt, through generations to come, for lifetimes not yet lived, just for what you did for me just now, in this second, without even thinking about our future.

Photo: *#1 Dreaming*
Credit: Natalia Mansurova.

Invitation to Ecstasy

A chance to see and not be seen
whirling ambrosia of musk and desire,
the room awash in
ever-changing colours of twilight.

Cascading visions of sensuality,
frequencies shimmering in the air
ingested lotus flowers
eyes half-closed
floating as if mist over water
gazing on to wetlands below.

The air was pierced
'Aaahhhhhhhhhh'
more than parted
with pleasures energetic tones,
human vibrations of flesh against skin,
sounds of power given.
Oohhhhhhhhh
power taken

Release
stuttered moans
sampled into the ever-fluid air
wood, carpet, bed, mattress, cloth, pillow, skin
hands touching bodies
mouths praying into other mouths . . .

Long moans
spilled across the room
as hips gathered gravity like
water poured onto skin,
as humans entered
each other . . .

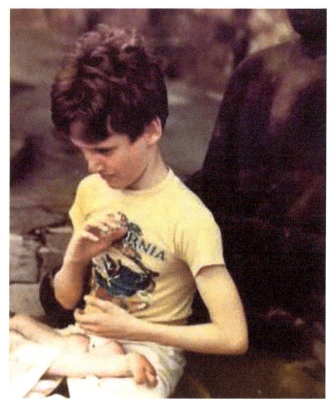

Photo: *Taro, 11 years, at the Temple of Borobudur, Indonesia.*
Credit: Saul Arbess

On Wealth

In a perfect world
to measure a man in muscle
is to reveal oneself a fool.

A man is measured in tears
in fear and failures,
in the humility to accept weakness
yet to move forward
in the face
of everything lost.

To measure a man in gold
is the ignorance of our species.
Every other beast of Earth knows
it cannot feed on metal
nor be kept warm by its yellowed hue.

Only man, proud man,
hides behind this Earth-scavenged
illusion. It is but in the blink of life's eye
that we discover
such gold is good for nothing
but a monument to a fool.

To measure a human in love, given and received,
in kindness and caring for those who have naught,
therein lies the strength of Titans.

Weigh not the gold in one's pockets;
it is dead weight, lead of a different
colour, pulling us into hellish depths.

Weigh instead how much one has lost,
given in service, in love,
in selfless acts
for only their own sake.

Then you will know the volume of true wealth.
Once we understand that riches
are the connections we make,
that wealth is one heart beating for the many,
and the true tycoons are those who
gave their last breath for love.

Once . . .
we had heroes who never
needed their names spoken.

They were our ideals.
If only I could live as I can feel,
as I can write,
I would die starving yet brimming with love,
not wallow alone on the very riches
that sank the world around me.

If we could leave this Earth
in the arms of those who wished
to leave with us, this would be
a planet of the truly wealthy,
where heaven is not
where we rise to
but where we rise from.

Just So

I set the carpets and rugs just so.
My love will walk softly when she enters
my room . . .

I roll back the sheets and fluff the pillows just so.
My love will lay softly when she enters
my room . . .

I fuss over artwork and candles beside the bed
just so my love will look pleased in her eyes
when she enters
my room . . .

I wipe away all traces of my sorrow
and any signs of my fear
so my love will feel peace
when she enters
my room . . .

Leave only beauty for your love;
show no sadness, longing
or pain
in my room . . .

Leave only beauty for my love;
whispering to her, I love you,
in my room . . .

Photo: *Taro lights a candle at Rainforest Pavilion temple at Wonderfruit festival in Thailand, December 2019.*
Credit: Florian Siempelkamp.

Midnight Mass

At night we travel
in majestic legions
through the inner valleys of
our soul systems.

Across shepherded fields
cosmic clouds exploding
with colours beyond
the spectrum of imagination.

Shades of beauty
trail comets,
paint the skies
in radiant hues of energy
made visible.

For all the moments
it roars into the night.
For a moment
we relinquish our bodies to entities unknown
but always welcome.

We dance with the spirits of those still here—
those who have gone—
those who will never leave—

We dance as if underwater
deep deep
into the blue-black mystery
that is the space . . .
between souls.

Highways for the collective hope
Love . . .
Anguish . . .
Compassion . . .

We need to channel,
to still, though never silence,
only return their source to ours
to cleanse any hurt,
to forgive and console,
care and caress.

We are the midnight dancers
in the dark open spaces.
We are the movers of light—
the blessed messengers of
the Dreamtime black light.

We are one fan unfolding
to blow a gentle breeze
of understanding
through the wind-whipped trees
that stretch into the future.

Loveissent.

Photo: Taro in *Club Mirror, Bali*.

The Three-Minute Poem

I wish it didn't come from so deep
that to write it down
diminishes me.

I wish I had a great writer's facility
to escape with loose-fitting words
tied together by a silver thread,
but all I've got is pages ripped
from a child's diary
held together by old man's hands
that shake so bad in rough weather
they can barely hold a drink or
a cigarette . . .

Still, I'm reading this poem
thinking about friends
who are addicts and prostitutes,
selling themselves to eat lotus flowers
and wear higher heels.
I'm wondering how it ever went this far.

Scared and excited,
not too comfortable in crowds,
always listening for the first whispers
of panic.

Still I'm reading this poem
and laughing
'cause somehow I did it:
I wrote a three-minute poem
that meant something to someone;
and I'll never be satisfied,
and I'll never be the same.

Photo: *Taro in Club Da Maria, Bali.*
Credit: Fiorenzo Nisi.

The Nightlife

For the road to here and now, and the people who paved the way, for friends, we have and friends we will meet along the way. For the freedoms and the freaks, geeks and wide-eyed daemons, we have stood for always and always will, for the Prom Queens, Drag Queens, Divas, Dilettantes, and Disco Dancers. For the leaders, the followers, and the music that brings us all together. For the purpose and the drive to keep doing what we do, and for the memories we create for the ones we love. For the old school and the new kids, and the place we can all be as one.

For the dance floors, the DJs, the sound systems, and the venues that, once built, they will come, and once closed, they will never forget.

For all nights and every day, and those who fill those times and bring us out to play.

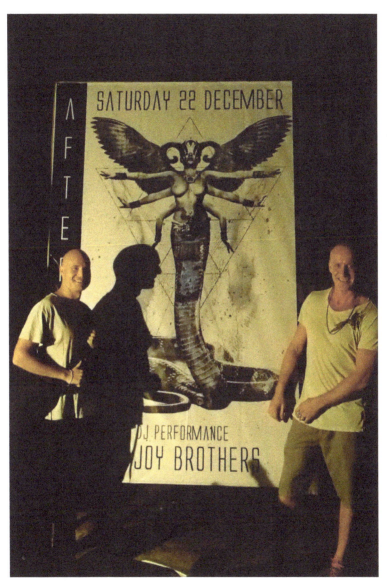

Photo: *Joy Brothers: Taro and Alexander, in front of promotional poster*
Credit: Dita Levins.

Photo: Taro as "Miss Behaving" in Maria Magdalena Club Bali, August 3, 2013. Credit: Fiorenzo Nisi.

Photo: Taro at DJ decks at Hacienda, Bali

Taro with champagne bottle

Photo: Taro at DJ decks in Jenja Club, Bali

Photo: Taro at DJ decks in Vault Club, Bali

Paris November 2015

I suppose it's all about degrees of separation. One hundred thirty-two people died last Friday in the Paris attacks. If anyone was within a couple of degrees of separation with any of them, they are devastated by this. There will be the friends of those directly affected; those people's families and associates will be brought that much closer to this horror. Thousands of people whose lives are irrevocably impacted, thousands of souls crying into this beautiful city. This is the ripple at the centre of the collective sorrow. Tears flow through this city now, watering the hearts of so many more inside it, in all of France and, from there, the rest of the world is drenched with the spray of this suffering.

It is Monday now; the excitement, fear, and fortitude of the collective outcry against the savagery is galvanising into a myriad of emotions. Life is settling into the realisation that a new day has dawned. France has been drawn deeper into this evil chess game with hidden powers moving all the pieces.

Security will be increased; fear, stress, and anxiety levels will be adjusted upward. Big Pharma companies will be making more money on the increased anxiety and sleep medications prescribed. The military-industrial complex will place more orders, drop more bombs, and in the spirit of aggression, ten will die for every one on Friday. Alcohol consumption will rise (all over the world) as people try to dull the sense of panic, loss, and hopelessness this trauma will bring about.

Paris will lose, the world will lose, and, but for a few arms dealers and corporations, there will be no winners. An eye for an eye will leave us all blind.

People will also write books because of what happened. They will paint pictures, make movies. Poetry will flow like tears, sculptures will come to life,

Dance will be salvation for some, and music will rise like a lotus from the mud of confusion.

Art will be another symptom of this stain on history. In the forge of emotion created last Friday, a million swords will be tempered. I pray they are used to cut through the artifice and entanglement of our sorrows, to battle the demons of hate, fear, and prejudice that threaten to poison all our hearts. I pray for those closest to the centre who lost someone they only just held moments before. I pray for the silenced here in Paris and around the world. Would that their anger, frustration, and despair could be transformed, expressed, expunged, and made a homage to those lost and a commitment to ending the conditions that create these horrible acts around the world.

We will all have to come to our own understanding of what is fundamentally wrong in society right now, of who is pushing the buttons and what are their real agendas.

The evidence is out there, but today is Monday, and in Paris, I am mourning with this city that I have only just visited, this once, but now feel in some way is a part of me. Paris, if this is your worst hour I have shared, then I cannot wait to come again because, even in the middle of this storm . . . you are so very beautiful.

> "*But Paris was a very old city, and we were young and nothing was simple there, not even poverty, nor sudden money, nor the moonlight, nor right and wrong nor the breathing of someone who lay beside you in the moonlight*".—Ernest Hemingway, *A Moveable Feast*

Baseball Bats to Vipassana

'From baseball bats to Vipassana', he said.
The look of shock
belied by the frown of confusion;
how could one go from one such extreme to the other?
He said it like he didn't already know the answer.
What am I if not the monster or myth of your making?
When did you think I would put down my sword to hand you a flower?

'Do not raise a golem from the ashes of your destruction,
then expect to know darkness from light,
immovable and irresistible even unto itself.
If in war you raise warriors
do not think they will sit to picnic after blood is let.'

Baseball bat or Vipassana, he said!
Both offer paths to the same,
divinity of silence.
The baseball bat is much faster.
When you ask me to feel one way
I feel that way.
When you ask me to move away,
I move away;
all you cannot do is un-ask me to do something.
You must live with the golems you create,
the destruction you cause.

Baseball bat or Vipassana, he said!
In the wake of the juggernaut
of your own design.
Never again be surprised by the tactics
you yourself employed . . .

Photo: *#2 Dreaming*
Credit: Natalia Mansurova.

Constriction (Plant Prohibition)

Life imitates the contradiction
of my soul's freedom versus my body's lack.
Prison, as a metaphor for who we are . . .
against who we want to be: . . .
A thin strip of glass set in a thick steel door,
the window to my soul?
No, the window to my cell . . .
A place where I am forced to look inwards,
to crack the egg that surrounds me,
with the illusion of freedom,
and touch that place that cannot be confined.
I, a monk who eats cookies,
a saint in an orange suit,
a humble man searching for truth in hard times.

White Knight

This is a story about the wild animals in my life that I could not avoid. Some were real and dangerous creatures that lurked in the shadows. Others are just metaphors for such creatures, lurking in my mind.

At this point in my life, I would say that the latter have been the most dangerous. One can survive encounters with any number of external life-threatening storms, fall in, tumble, flail and flounder until you have been spat out the other side, still having the memory to count as a strength (or perhaps live in fear of forever). The storm that lives inside, driving like a punch-drunk prize fighter behind the wheel of a stolen car, that is the one storm that pushes out all the others along the way.

A multiple murderer, convicted of very few of the killings he told me he had committed, once asked me if I thought he was going to go to hell when he died. That would be a heavy question at the best of times, but when you are sharing a ten-by-twelve-foot cell with a man who has just confided in you that he has killed a dozen people (that he can remember), it's a question that definitely requires some deep contemplation—or, at the very least, a moment of pause.

It was my Gordian knot of sorts—so much more than a simple question and answer; more an immovable object meeting with an irresistible force. Logic would dictate that my answer should be vague and non-confrontational, but logic had gone out the window when my old life had ended; instinct was now in play, that, or oblivion.

To describe this cellmate of mine is difficult. It is a memory now, and, knowing how my mind works, memories will sometimes exaggerate themselves until sometimes they are hardly recognisable.

His name is White Knight; no other option is given, which gives you some insight into his politics. Regarding race, he is pure Aryan Brotherhood, one of the old-school white supremacists who ran the joint in the '70s and '80s but now have only moderate 'strength'; though, what they have, they hold fast to, and it isn't questioned. These men in charge are intelligent, psychotic, violent animals. White Knight is one of them. His body is a motley map of tattooed chaos: swastikas peppered about with no real order. A map of California, made of prison bars, with his face looking out, covers one calf. His arms, covered in images of flames and violence, contain numbers pricked in with staples dipped in ink, made of the ash of burnt chess pieces mixed with shampoo; each tat a nightmare recorded on his skin forever. He wears death, Satan, and an image of Hitler proudly with no remorse. Yet, from a lifetime in prison and committing horrors in the few times he was out, he knows it is his uniform for protection. Underneath, way deep, he is just a man, afraid of what he doesn't have control over. Thankfully, this man decides that understanding me will be more fruitful than smashing me.

Physically, he is commanding, under his sweater of tattoos. On his grizzled face, he has the skin of a man accustomed to sleeping drunk in rail cars and parking lots, of waking up bruised and beaten with no memory of why; yet, the body of a hardened soldier betrays the first dazed impression. He has trained in prison yards, street fights raised him, blood and hate were his parents. A year on either side of fifty, by my guess, he has long enough white hair to tie in a knot, giving him a sort of trailer park samurai look. His eyes, deep-set pits, with frighteningly luminous blue orbs, simmer within. He wears the handlebar moustache that is trademark for bad guys and wannabes, allowing it to fall off at his jawline and finish thick and full on the neck. He is a force, respected by blacks, whites, and guards alike, simply because he moves and speaks and believes he rules the prison, and you know that the second you lay eyes on him.

I think that questions of eternal damnation, of heaven and hell or other such BIG topics, are probably best avoided when locked in a room, unsupervised with a 250-pound white supremacist serial killer. The answer, in the end, came, simple and divine, at the same moment, but the friendship that ensued because of it was most complex. So that was the knot, and this was how I cut it.

> 'Hey man, a life of killing, of travelling rail cars, drunk on death and whatever will erase it, blacking out and waking up in other people's blood with blurry memories of murder, that is as close to hell as you're going to get; it won't get worse from death; no God worth believing in is that cruel'.

These words emerged somehow from a twenty-four-year-old school dropout with a major in kung fu and an advanced degree in bong hits.

There was also a slow dream, one that often came to me in those days . . . perhaps a slow-motion dream is what I mean, like a wide-angle Panavision shot that is closing in from somewhere in outer space to a tiny point on Earth. In the dream, first I see the planet barely visible beneath layer upon layer of cloud formation and fragmented light. Blues and whites swirl amidst dark landmasses, two-dimensional, as if clouds and oceans and land all sit on one plane. Then I enter the ether, the area where nothing and nowhere becomes something and somewhere. There is no time, no markers or shapes that seem familiar. It is Earth only because that is all I know, yet it has elements of all I do not know spread throughout. I pass through clouds and air, and they feel no different.

I am not falling, not flying, just observing, as if through a camera lens or perhaps a microscope. When I break through the cloud cover, the whole Earth is before me, stripped raw and barren, as if it has all become dust and desert and is slowly shifting itself into the oceans, which have turned the colour of arterial blood for a thousand miles off any shore. Still moving, now even faster, I can smell the dryness of the air infused with dust and smoke. The crust of this burnt Earth comes at me fast; I wait for impact and death. Still, at the last second, I am moving horizontally across the surface at speed, winding through valleys, over mountains, all charred with heat scars burnt into them, desperately looking anywhere for any sign of life—there is none.

Slowly, I start to decelerate from this tumultuous journey from outer space to this sand-whipped land that might have once been my Earth, but no longer resembles it. Then, in the far distance, a single figure stands, praying to the sky, with hands clasped and raised to heaven, hands wrapped in swathes of earth-coloured linen, material ripped perhaps from grain sacks and tied over dirty white skin for protection.

The lens that is me moves in slowly and methodically as if, somehow, I can be seen as I approach, and do not want to excite or scare this last soul on Earth. He turns his gaze from the sun and looks into my eyes with empty sockets that somehow stream with tears. It is my face, and I mouth the words.

"Why am I here?"

WHAM!!! Every morning wakes me with the subtlety of a shotgun full of hate fired into my sleeping face. There's no escape: days full of boredom that resemble nightmares, and nights full of dreams that resemble hell. I buy meds out of the throats of schizos. After the nurse looks away, they spit them up and give them to me for a chocolate bar. A week's worth of three men's meds guarantees me a few hours of blank static space. Later, they are wheeled out in straitjackets, drool running down their chins. I have to make something here—draw out divinity where none seems to exist. Prison is not so much a mechanism to lock away the body, as it is a tool to break apart the soul.

I was on a sinking ship that never quite went under—constant panic just below the surface, boiling rage, blood-red eyes, veins popping in my neck. This is how I lived every day, and how I dreamt every night. I could not change the waking day, but I would try and change my nights. Dreams are within my flesh, and there lies what little space exists over which I still had governance.

Days in hard time passed slowly, even with my new friend White Knight to talk with. We play chess. In our little honeycomb of hell, the chessboard has no white knight on it—that stays stuck above our cell door, untouched by guards or killers. We spend hours working out together, push-ups, sit-ups, bench dips on chairs, and jumping jacks—anything that requires no equipment because that's all gone now. Too many heads crushed under fitness weights, we now have to fill garbage bags with water and tie them to toilet brushes, then lift them until they break, and finally we have to switch to cleaning up our mess.

I am aware of a sense of protection that this man has bestowed on me, but equally, he treats me as if I have brought him not just friendship but salvation. I am aware that he is fire, and I am moving way too close, but sometimes fire seems like the best thing to play with in the absence of anything else. I have become a spiritual arsonist of sorts. Staying strong with him is as close to an extinguisher as I will ever be.

He teaches me the rules of engagement, where not to be, and how to get there quickly, if needed. Introductions are made, and, at my insistence, it is made clear that we are as divided on our politics as strongly as we are united in our friendship. I am the son of a Jewish father and a Buddhist mother. This, I let be known. In here, I am far more afraid of killing my own spirit than of someone else doing the job for me.

> 'One day, we will have nothing to stand on, but what we have stood for until now'.

I meditate on that quotation, and to me, it rings true, even in the face of the high levels of hatred that permeate this place. Now, let's get this straight for everyone, I am a white boy who despises Aryan Brotherhood, opposes racism and has friends of every colour. I am pretty much trusted by no one, but kept alive, perhaps mostly for entertainment, and surely because, there is a mystery to me that some would like to unlock, and others are afraid to fuck with.

> *'One day, we will have nothing to stand on but what we have stood for till now'.*

Believe in something; even if it's just a sentence that makes sense; it may save your life one day. I read as much as possible, anything. Books are torn into chapters and spread throughout the prison; while the chance of ever completing a book is small to none, every page is a sanctuary, an escape, time spent, not hard or hurt or worse. Words start to take on such significance, simple phrases one can stop and ponder. I am meditating on sentences, on words and structures, the cadence of a paragraph. How it shifts and sings and rolls across the mind, the artistry that went into it (or, all too often, the lack of it).

Even the bad stuff is inspirational. I am reaching something here, inside walls surrounded by walls, surrounded by fences, with men who carry guns pointed at me. I am grasping for freedom and understanding what it truly means. Arm-curling garbage bags full of water with murderers in a dark metal room is getting me closer to something sacred than I have ever been.

What are these tidal waves I am releasing? I asked for change, but am I ready? There seems to be words and moments that release floods of vivid memories. I feel my eyes dilate, neurons fire, electrical impulses run codes through grey matter, and life unfolds like a visual, auditory, immediate, drug-free hallucination. These memories sometimes come slowly—building steam like a train picking up speed as it lunges into my consciousness like a perfect mainline rush. They hang like mist over the water, ghostly apparitions that slowly fade, begging me to decode them before 'now' time slips back into the forefront.

These memories bring pause, bring moments of replay and suggestion. The past offers as many questions as answers; duality is always maintained in nature. Ah! —the difficulty in sustaining a natural state of being in an increasingly unnatural environment.

I am asking questions meant for mystics on mountaintops. I am asking them to walls and steel bars and . . . I am getting answers.

Photo: *Getting answers*
Credit: Fiorenzo Nisi.

Hard Choice Fast

I had a friend; one I miss often and think of frequently. We met suddenly on the yard in some prison, in some hell, somewhere in the middle of nowhere. We had been almost ninety days in solitary since, in our own personal version of Icarus, we flew into the sun with wax wings, diamond eyes, marmalade hands, got burned, and were separated when our "co-conspiracy" was discovered. I'll never forget seeing Ed. We were both broken. The type of broken where, to have something in the world to do, a man separates into a thousand little parts, names each, has them talk to one another. The type of broken where you realise that the man who designed your cell has thought more about suicide than you ever could because there are no options provided short of bashing your own skull to a pulp on a wall.

We had been rounded up; our few possessions thrown into a cardboard box. After a serious examination (that would take a book to describe), we are shepherded in chains, by armed men, to a bus that brings us to a concrete field. There we are left in the hot sun, with a crowd of murderers and their ilk, lined up on a chain fence inside another chain fence in the middle of a space surrounded by walls thirty feet high, and guard towers in all four corners containing men with guns pointed at us. Ed and I spot each other immediately but stay quiet. The second we were as sure as possible that the towers are not going to open fire, we quietly rejoice at seeing each other. As soon as guards lock the fence gate, without a word, men begin to approach us—evil-looking men, with swastikas tattooed on their chests, arms, and legs, and other symbols covering most of their flesh, some including large portions of their faces.

Hard choice fast; that's life in prison. We are being asked to join gangs, accept tobacco, chocolate bars, stamped letters. The loot is offered thick and fast; swiftly it became obvious that the offers come only from whites and Latinos. We, motley crew of post-traumatic stressed newbies, are only being approached by our own colour. Being a major in philosophy and, all around, probably one of the smartest minds I know, Ed got it first. He thinks we must now be in some mating ritual, with gangland overtones. He thinks, and I concur, that to accept any gifts offered will likely mean purchase and eventual ownership of our anuses. We politely decline all offers from tattooed Nazis, try to slink backwards into the chain mail, and become invisible. Decent tactic, total failure. Noticing our obvious discomfort, one guy in the group that surrounds us, tells us it's okay, we can accept gifts without any fear of payback debts (sad to say his name eludes me, perhaps because non-threats are stored in a more easily forgotten memory bank). Different colours apparently help their own, out of pity, recognising that they have all entered in a state like ours.

We smoke till we are dizzy, and laugh for the first time in months. The celebration is brief. Next, we face the difficult task of trying to decide how to navigate the cellblock we have just been tossed into. A hundred men on fifty double bunks, slightly secluded open toilets, showers to accommodate twenty at a time. The prison is separated into Bloods and Crips sections for the black gangs, North and South for the Latinos. Whites can go anywhere. All whites, to the last one, white supremacists, Aryan Brotherhood. We are supposed to bunk down with Crips, Nortenos and a gang of Charlie Manson wannabees, with a hive mentality of hate and superiority, despite the obvious fact that they are inferior, outnumbered, and half the size of most of the overwhelmingly black population. We make no move to join the white brothers, and get looks from confused, distrustful, angry eyes. You are expected to flock to your colour in prison because your colour will protect you—but what if your colour wears Swastikas and admires Hitler (even though no one I met really had any idea who he was!) We are vexed. Only a few hours have passed, time for hard choices again.

Mealtime arrives, we queue for food, watch as colours sit segregated. Tables for eight, colour segregated, even, it seems, age or maybe seniority is an issue. Old black men at one table, middle age (meaning twenty in this place) whites at another. The hard Latin leaders sit only four to their tables, and, throughout the meal, invite people for 'talks'. We reach the front of the queue, in the process of having our slop shovelled onto our plastic trays, decide we will not sit with the whites. Better to live on our feet than die on our knees is the idea, though at the time our thoughts are simply 'we cannot live like that'. We avoid tables full of racist rednecks, mostly meth heads, who are clearly outnumbered and outpowered on all sides by the multitude of other races surrounding them. We take our food and walk slowly to the table of old black men. We sit and begin to eat tentatively, watching each other's backs. We chose the older men thinking that being older they might be wiser and understand our dilemma, maybe more so than any of the others. In retrospect, we should have remembered what we had known for years: age does not necessarily guarantee wisdom. This situation provides a firm reminder. An apparently wise-looking old man next to us says,

> *'Looks like you muthafuckas is sitting at the wrong table—peckerwoods over there'.*

He points to the tables where we had decided not to sit. At this point, my story will sound foolish. Truth is, I cannot believe the gamble I took. I don't expect anyone else to believe it. This story, up to now, has been to introduce you to the character who next steps in . . .

I remember being young, riding my skateboard, Walkman plugged into my ears at full blast. It was mostly punk music, Dead Kennedys, GBH, and darker local shit released on tape cassettes outta punk rock gigs. My bro, Paul, gave me a Niggers With Attitude CD. The clarity and intensity of this black music from the streets of

L.A. struck a chord. Being middle class, from a loving family, in an almost exclusively white neighbourhood, I had found little to rebel against. When NWA offered me their ghetto lives, their 'be strong or die trying' attitude and 'fuck authority' shouted loud, I loved it! It made me feel marginalised, as if I too had fought a life of oppression and clawed to the top on crack rocks and jump shots. I remembered some words from 'Fuck the Police' - judge to defendant,

> 'The jury has found you guilty of being a redneck, white bread, chicken shit motherfucker!'

It was raw, hard, from the underground, the first gangster rap I had ever heard; its anger fuelled me.

Perhaps that same anger bubbled to the surface ten years later when that old man told me to go sit with a bunch of evil-looking, strung-out Nazis—implying that they were my people. I took that first verse of NWA and told him, loud enough for all to hear, that there was no way I was going to sit with those 'white bread, chicken shit motherfuckers'.

The silence after those words was deafening. I had played an almost impossible hand with the hope that somebody large and black in that prison felt the same way I did about an obscure underground rap song from ten years prior. All eyes were on me and Ed; people at both white and black tables began to rise. What seemed like an eternity, probably seconds, passed, then there was a thunderous crash and the biggest, meanest looking black man I had ever seen smashed his fist into the table and shouted

> 'If these boys don't wanna eat with those pieces of shit then they can eat with me, and any muthafucka got a problem with that can come over to my bunk later and get raped!'

So ferocious was this man's appearance and demeanour that not a peep is heard from anyone in this room full of one hundred inmates. All slowly sit back down and resume eating.

I have gone all the way here to introduce you to this character, a real person, a friend, and truly one of the most knowledgeable, defiant, strong, empowering, evil men I have ever met. Known as Weasel, he is six foot eight, has six bullet holes scarred into his brown skin, and 'Africa's Finest' tattooed down the back of each arm, with crossed spears on his elbows. Across his back in gothic text, six inches high, horrifically torn by scars from police bullets but still legible, is written 'GRAPE STREET CRIPS'. His hair a massive 'fro' worn each day in just two braids standing straight out of his head in opposing directions. He is the toughest gang member I saw in all the hundreds, perhaps thousands, I met inside who made anyone you have seen in the movies look like the actors they are. It was with him that Ed and I subsequently honed our chess skills, had some of the most insightful conversations, and made diabolical plans, never to be carried out. He was the reason that we were never fucked with for all our three month and eleven days in this ever-changing cell block of midway to the pen murderers. It's hard to imagine he is still alive, but equally hard to conceive he is dead. If he ever reads this, or anyone who knows him does, please tell him, 'Thank you', from Ed and me.

Photo: *Taro, Ed, and fellow inmates.*

New Beginnings

Reset, reset, reset . . . breathe
Rain spills
happy tears of goddesses . . .
blanketing the hungry dry earth
with succulent promise.

The Earth spreads
her arms and legs
taking heaven into her
as a lover . . .

Sky gods
beat thunder drums
electric clouds clap
vivid lightning strikes
Earth resetting, replenishing, rebirthing.

Roots swell
with the blood of the planet
rushing into them.
Stems arise from dry earth,
blossoms tremble
on the edge of explosion.

Dreams of vibrant blooms
spin like galaxies
in the minds of lovers everywhere
While birds and bees
hide in their safe

complex palaces
amongst the trees
and forests of Earth
waiting for the celestial skies
to open their crystal blue eyes,
pour sunlight, mist, and the smell of
rich planetary passion
across the elated,
aroused, vibrant,
sated lands.

Now is the time for seeds to be planted
pollen to carry in the wind
on the feet and in the mouths
of angels

Now is the dawn of new days
new beginnings
the start of a new set of endings
waiting to be discovered and waiting to begin

Life . . .
Perpetual cyclical
Beautiful
Life . . .
Silence

Photo: Taro in a jungle river in Sumatra
Credit: Alexander Arbess-Joy

Just Breathe

'Just breathe', said my goddess, only a moment ago,
'deep into the heart, so the air's rich wind lights up your soul'.

'But why?' I asked, 'when I find you in the still place between breaths.

'The silent place deep below
Wind
Water
Fire
Air
are all part of your shell', she said.
'Stand on the shore when the fire burns behind you.
Om to the ocean,
give thanks to the air for living in your mouth,
for you living at all.
Each breath is a prayer going into your lungs,
each prayer a song from the universe,
just for you'.
Amen, Inshallah, Namaste, Om Swastiastu, Mitakuye Oyasin,
Loveissent.

Transmission

This is the timeless tale of a dancer,
a DJ, a reluctant shaman—
the legend of an ancient sorceress
that recognised him
and the Goddess that is coming in to empower
on a mission to save planet Earth.

With a cast of conscious individuals, untrained masters, and
unsung heroes who were moved by the story,
inspired by the frequencies and
touched by the Goddess,
this is a story for all good humans.
This is our story . . .

Photo: *#3 Waking up!*
Credit: Natalia Mansurova

Kannon

I have wanted a new tattoo for years now, always searching for the image, and the feeling I would wear forever. There was one that I entertained putting on my skin—it was from an illustration for a bible made by William Blake entitled *Rout of the Rebel Angels*.

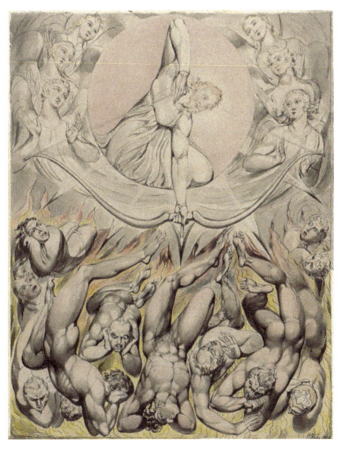

Rout of the Rebel Angels: William Blake.

It held an intensity and a feeling of my life, as I have felt both a rebel angel storming heaven and a warrior fighting back the storm of rebels that threaten my universe. Of course, I intended to change the piece somewhat, make it less denominational; the angels would represent things I have conquered as well as things I have allowed into my life. The image routing the angels, with a bow and arrow from within a fiery sun, was to be a cross between me and Saul (the father I chose, and the man I will become), bearded, muscular, and intense. Now I only needed the right person to put it on me—not such an easy task. I know some of the finest artists in the world. I party with them, hang out with them, and call myself friends with many, but none of whom I knew possessed enough of what I truly respect in a person to allow them to be the hand that marks me for life - which is something I must remember.

Then, one day, while getting my hair cut, a friend walks in with this big, scary-looking *gaijin* and introduces him as Clay Decker, builder of the finest tattoo guns and artist to the stars.

We end up going for a beer, and I hear his story. An American with a rough background who found himself through art, especially Japanese art for which his skill is so great that he is a favourite inscriber of one of Japan's most revered tattooists, Hiroyoshi 111, a man who is considered a national treasure, and whose work is worn by the upper echelons of the *Yakuza*.

So, here is a man, like myself, a foreigner in love with a land on the other side of the planet from the one on which they had arrived, dedicated to life as an artist, and respected even more in his adopted land than at home. He is a nice man, a little goofy and genuinely good, derived perhaps from allowing most of the bad to pass through him in the rough years. We feel kindred; my tattoo is put on the design table and scheduled to be inked on my right arm, shoulder to wrist. We work for many hours on the design until finally, after a lot of drafts, Clay produces a powerful piece of work, and I am scheduled for the next day to have it done.

Photo: *Hiroyoshi 111*   Photo: Clay Decker
                         Credit: Clay Decker

That night, I go to a big trance party and dance as if possessed, open as if no one is watching, shedding the blanket of conformity that has slowly descended on Tokyo days. There are some doses of LSD involved. As I danced, first came the sensation that everybody else stopped moving, while I am still dancing; though the music is silent, the rhythm still moves inside me. Then a red light hits me in the third eye, and Quan Yin, or Kannon, as she is known in Japan, descends on this beam of light. She is dancing and telling me that I must not get my intended tattoo, that it will throw my life out of balance and cause ruin, but there is a tattoo I should have that will bring balance and peace to my life. Then I am dancing behind myself, looking at my own back, and she is on my back dancing beautifully with her flowers, and I know that is what I must get inked, and I know why.

All my life, I have lived around this image; we travelled under it in Asia, there are statues and temples to her everywhere, my home has always been filled with her smiling face, my mother prays to her for my soul, as well as the planet. I know that every time I see her, I am reminded of your smile, knowing she has always been there in our heart and will make others smile. She will balance my yang and remind me to live right, and remind me of a mother who has loved me with all her heart, all my life. I am alive, I am intrinsically good, and happiness is my birth right. I knew right away that I could put a smile on your face with this tattoo, mother; the other would have made you cry, and that alone was enough.

The next day, I walked into the studio and announced that I was afraid we had to scrap the old tattoo as I need this one, as large as possible, on my back. I tell Clay the story, and he answers

'No problem, friend; LSD saved my life and we can't question spirit'.

Since the day it was completed, I have felt her questioning my actions, providing soft advice and gentle council. When I dance, I feel her dancing, and people stand behind me to watch her move. I am gentler, more feminine when needed, and my strength is in staying my hand. I am regarded with intense confusion, but utter respect by Japanese men in the *onsen*—Taro, with white skin and Kannon on his back. When people ask what my tattoo is, and if I do not have time or wish to explain all this, I simply reply

'My mother'.

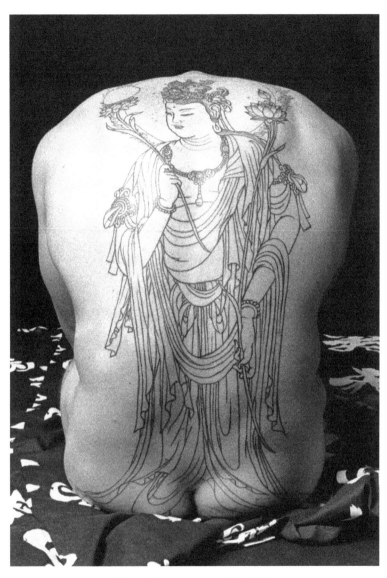

Photo: *Kannon tattoo on Taro's back*
Credit: Clay Decker

I Miss Tokyo

When you miss something
you make it real,
in your heart's door,
in your soul's window.
When you really love something
you make it real ,
in your centre.

I miss Tokyo

Blacklight streets whispering,
from one structure to the next,
halogen fire lamps,
lighting up sumo matches on damp clay.
Vendors selling drinks and meat in the darkness
around each viewing box.

I miss Shibuya

The back alleys
where we traded Gudan cards
and toys we didn't understand,
drank warm sake from clay jugs
and laughed with drunken geishas on their way home.
Ommmmmmm

I miss Fucking
in the back allies of Roppongi,
under the monsoon rains.
The taste of skyscraper-kissed raindrops

dripping off your lips
like tears from heaven
to wash away my pain.

I miss Sakura
in the moat
rowing our boat under
fertile, plump cherry blossoms
hanging outside the stone walls
of the royal palace,
singing Italian words
I don't understand
with an English accent.

I miss the freeways
of Yokohama.
Electric-powered motor paths stacked ten levels high,
the rainbow bridge at night
spitting cars out of each end
from double loops spiralling
away from each other.

I miss the feel of your head
against my chest
the size of an large apple,
purring like a baby dragon
while you sleep.

I miss the weight and heat
of you in my arms,
in my hands,
curled around my lungs,
one hand on my heart,
head bowed.

That is the silence
I will never forget,
never surrender,
and always, always
seek to meet.

Om Swastiastu,
Inshallah,
Amen,
Namaste,
Mitakuye Oyasin,
Loveissent.

Photo: *Taro with Kosei in Tokyo*

Photo: *Taro, Tokyo*

Photo: *Taro with Justin in Tokyo*

Come Home Now, Child

First word brings a tear
knowing that what will be written
is so beautiful,
so blessed.

Even angels cried to imagine
the genesis breath
of that child they dreamed,
dreamed with all their love.

Silent invocation of creation
wanting to emerge
from the cavernous myriad of paths
they have shared.

Come, child,
into this world we will to you—
come dance in the light of love
never painted with anything
but kindness
caring
compassion
Joy.

We wait here in the imagining—
in the in-between place
of lovers
dreamers
dancers in the night.

There are arms to hold you here
against hearts that beat with your blood.
There are eyes that shut now only to see your face
in the gentle flicker of dreams.

Great halls of light inside our souls
sing for your arrival,
great ships sail into the heavens
to herald your return.

We have travelled so far to find you.
Through lifetimes
we have searched our hearts' desire
only to find
all paths lead to you.

Come cry, come laugh,
come cuddle and play,
come stand on the shores of forever
with us . . .
Skip stones into the future;
giggle as the sun hits your face.

Come sleep between us;
let us whisper
our love
forever for you,
forever . . .
for you.

Photo: *Dita welcomes daughter Alexa.*
Credit: Taro Zion Joy.

Fatherhood

This time at night's start, when the day completes, and parents sometimes find that moment of grace where the world suddenly slows down, even grinds to a momentary halt, when they for an hour, minute, second can reflect, often unwind, diffuse, as if finally unbecoming. My daughter sleeps with such peace. I can only imagine that I once knew what that felt like.

This is Satori for me, closer to the goddess than drugs, pain, or meditation has ever gotten me. It is in servitude to my little goddess that I have for a moment each day been allowed to gaze at myself with something that resembles pride, but, in actuality, is gratitude bordering on true liberation of my soul, a oneness with such clarity that it exists nowhere else, but in my heart as it beats when I am parenting.

In truth, I have done nothing for myself and yet feel to have eaten a feast with the gods. In laying all that is me aside to further the experience of this tiny, fragile being who has allowed me to be teacher, provider, protector, incubator, and incantation of love's design, I am so completely enabled. It is as if I am god serving god and being allowed to see through my own mortal eyes why true love is immortal and exists only in the giving away of all of oneself. I am forgiven for the journey thus far and allowed the privilege of the journey to come. I fear even writing it down diminishes it, but if I can capture one tiny scrap of the essence of this love I try to describe, then my day, my life, has not been for nought.

If I were to ever be remembered for anything, I would want it to be that a child could love me enough to sleep in my arms, to run to me when afraid, and speak my name to find strength—everything else has just been grist for the mill.

Grist for the mill. I am proud of nothing; pride has been forsaken for love, and I lay down tonight so full of reverence for these few fleeting moments alone with a sleeping angel.

Photo: *Taro welcomes daughter Alexa.*
Credit: Dita Levins.

I Want for my daughter

I want . . .
I want to give
MUSIC!!

That hits the hips
Heart! Head!
All at once in an explosion
that reminds us
all things are beautiful.

I want . . .
I want to give
WORDS!!

That light a fire
in the chest
burning understanding
of love into the soul's
cellular memory.

I want . . .
I want to give
IDEAS!!

That set off fireworks
in the mind
sending fingers of
excited flame,
reaching for the limits of our
inner solar system.

I want
want to give
HAPPINESS!!

That sends us dancing into the
endless nights . . .
of our imagination . . .

Photo: *Taro 'launches' Alexa*

First Breath

First breath—
cold mountain air.
Sunlight flickers through her hair
like a strobe light in heaven.

We ride the lift slowly,
holding hands.
Crisp fresh air fills our lungs,
pushing oxygen like tiny dancing nymphs
into our souls
filling our blood and bodies
with the mountain's prana.

We become the wind whipping
through the jagged peaks surrounding us.

We become the spray of snow off the trees below us.
Sounds are of the skids and curves of children's first turns,
the squeals of delight
the shouts of defeat,
the cries of the hurt.
We are on our boards now,
riding into the future.

First contact, as we touch down
from chair to frozen earth.
Holding hands,

we lean forward like dropping into a ramp—
this feeling you know
or you do not.

We are moving now
on the surface of icy, frozen clouds,
carving just barely with one foot out so as to
STOP!

Time to lock-in—
boots to board and bindings bound.
We connect with our devices;
we sit side by side, staring into an ever-white infinity.

I have been told that snowboarding is
a dance with a mountain.
This is what I will teach my girl—
to dance with the snow,
dance with the air,
dance with life,
live it in every second.
This is what I teach my girl.

She leads and I follow behind
like a great bird hovering over its offspring.
She is my life,
blood flowing in my veins;
she is every beat of my heart,
every breath in my mouth.

She asked me to
take her to the mountain;
now I must give her to the mountain.
Praying, she holds her gently
as a goddess would—
her firstborn daughter.

Praying, she allows her
to play
to pray
to dance
on her loving slopes.

The mountain, who has always been my friend,
my tutor, my master,
the mountain trained me
for the struggles
that can be life.

The mountain I know—
capable of hard lessons forced,
of delivering pain
as easily as it delivers ecstasy.

To set my heart free
into the abyss is the ultimate prayer.

To see her run wild
on the face of raw nature is the greatest gift.

She flies like an icicle released—
liquid and confident,
focused and free.

She is all that is good and pure and right in me.
Now charging a mountain,
feeling her body move against its might,
owning her place in the world.

Praying to the Earth
Sky
Heaven
from which she is made.

She is an angel
like none I have ever seen.

Photo: *Taro and Alexa off the mountain*

The Door (for my mother)

The door—
I always leave
open for you.
Some nights
I sit in silence
anticipating your arrival
as a flower anticipates the sun.

The door I always leave open for you
is in my chest
and in my home.

Wildflowers sing
five sisters dance for you
each time you step inside.

Your name is a prayer
in my mouth
I utter with every breath.

The door I leave open for you
opens a thousand doors unseen—
each one
a myriad of visions
of futures . . .
fates . . .
freedoms . . .
and failures . . .
All lives lived by us inside my soul.

I know you know—
I have always trusted you were there,
in the open door that leads to my heart,
in the unfathomable reaches
of my deepest heart's desire,
in the truth inside me.
There you have always stood,
my radiant goddess,
my teacher,
my faith,
in love.

Photo: *Taro and mom, Penny, in Ibiza, circa 1976.*

With This Feather

I fan smoke across our future—
smoke-filled, with a father's wisdom—
burnt echoes of a strong lived history.

With this feather I call down the ancestors of my one King—
dance with your past,
forget about your future—
it will find you soon enough.

Pray where you stand,
look to all directions;
I am as sacred as the last.

With this feather from my father, I paint our names
upon our skin.
With this feather from my father
I open all doors to let you in.
Thanks to all the ancestors and agents of the night,
love to all the living who see with second sight!

A feather from my father
has given all of this.
A prayer for my father,
my returning
all his gifts.

Inshallah,
Amen,
Namaste,
Om,
Swastiastu,
Mitakuye Oyasin.
Loveissent.

Photo: *Saul Arbess -70th birthday in Raja Ampat.*
Credit: Alexander Arbess-Joy.

When You Speak a Word to Someone

When you speak a word to someone
you can cast a spell.
Words, liquid magic,
pours from your centre.

They wrap around a soul who listens;
they paint universes in the mind
Success . . .
Betrayal . . .
Love
Hate

Be careful of the spells you cast;
be careful of the universes you create.
To make a future with a word is easy—
but unmaking?
Unmaking
is a much harder thing.

Inshallah, Namaste, Om Swastiastu, Mitakuye Oyasin.

Loveissent.

I Hear the Universe in You

I hear the universe in you,
feel the blood flowing into your skin,
feel ravenous streams of energy
trying to be expelled in you.

Each time I try to dive in,
I hear chants, songs, hymns
underneath—
so many silent screams . . .

In you, I see the universe unfold,
beauty inked upon your skin.
Soundless nights call to us,
in a language unknown . . .

A thousand planets
follow you;
a thousand planets fall.

I can see the universe in you
calling me back home . . .

There were stars
we set into the sky;
poems, prayers, and smoke
we held eternal
as do or die . . .

There are these prayers we send into the sky
of Life
Love
Unity . . .
and a souls need to fly.

We send them now with gratitude
in humble tears of Joy.

Promises, prayers, and platitudes—
we grant and share and
promise not to cry.
It's difficult to watch the future from just one seat—
you must change hats to see ahead;
one man must be
Seer
Soldier
King
Hermit
in the same breath.

Choose wisely what you wear into battle,
choose wisely what you stand for,
as this will be the only ground you have to stand upon.
Pray to your goddess,
listen to your dreams—
fairy armies gather for you
on the blacklight bridge, the ecstasy of which
you have barely dared to dream.

Thank you for your service, thank you for your Joy;
bless this world around us,
bless each girl and boy.
Namaste, Om Swastiastu,
Loveissent.

Photo: Taro and Alexa give thanks
Credit: Jen Li.

Burning Down Libraries

We drove into each other like two trains colliding.
It was our very first secret catastrophe—
the genesis of our unused dreams,
setting the stage for emotional blasphemies to come.

Now, as we pick and pillage each other's bones for meat to hold onto,
we barely notice the earth below us scorches,
the ground behind us salting the last remnants of our hearts.

Breaking,
every time we turn and leave each other like strangers.

With no ground untravelled, we wander,
back and forth across each other,
oblivious to what we trample beneath our feet.

Can't you see?
Our angel is exhausted
from dragging beds between empty rooms
so that we might land somewhere soft.

Should we fall again into love?

This place is a mausoleum—
a cemetery of unfinished stories,
half-truths, and long-forgotten lies.

This place is a heart—
it has taken a lifetime to fill,
and, like all great collections,
will take only a few people,
a large box,
and a long day to pack up.

A deep hole might suffice,
but I would see this library we built, burn,
so that some smoke might escape
so that some part of this
might ascend.
The rest could then simply disappear.
Ashes to angels,
we all fall down.

A Perfect Storm

Like being invited into a perfect storm,
the perfection of annihilation—
a golden ticket to the chocolate factory.

Where words fail me,
memories will not.
I will finish with a precious few;
this will be one of them.

Bodies, like landscapes stretching into each other,
passions shared, like children in the garden of Eden,
limits, like time or depth, cease to exist.

Suddenly, I am whole; whole
pleasure measures gratitude. I fall off
the Earth and sky above it—

I meet my angel rising, my banished star descends;
we slap asses, like cheeky brothers in a brothel;
we are the alpha and omega of pleasures—
bookends in the library of perfection.

Four Truths of a First Burn

DUKKHA *(The truth of suffering)*

Sitting with an old friend at a cafe having a light lunch, I received a phone call I never truly thought I would ever receive. Thanking my lawyer profusely, I hung up, told my friend excitedly, '*I can go to the States again; I can see my little girl, meet her teachers, be part of her life. I am so happy*'. My friend, Romeo, was excited too. '*Zion*', he said, '"*you can also come to Burning Man in three weeks and help my friend build a pyramid in the desert!*'.

The truth hadn't sunk in yet . . . though it would.

I will never forget that I was not allowed to travel on one-third of the Earth's landmass for half my adult life. Nearly a year of my life was spent behind bars for a crime that is one no longer one on either side of the border—transporting a plant. A thing like that affects you in all sorts of subtle ways and eventually becomes part of you, even if you don't realise it—though, I did. You become an exile, a *persona non grata*, a pariah in some circles (mostly the circles inside your mind in which you pace, trying to reconcile what happened). It will be something you joke about, something you have a thousand ways to diminish, disregard, or straight-up lie about, but it will affect you.

Build a pyramid at Burning Man'—why not? It seemed right in line with my love of Grand Entrances and endless desire not to be even remotely 'normal' (as if such a state of being even exists). Still in shock from the news of my 'return from exile', I agreed on the spot, and, bless Romeo, he got to work right away securing all the right tickets and paperwork for a 'volunteer' (in this case, someone paying less than full price was considered a volunteer) to get on the early arrival crew for Burning Man 2017.

We showed up at night, and although it wasn't nearly the luxury described in their flashy web pages and well-shot interior views, the camp seemed nice to me (having never seen anything with which to compare it). It had more the feel of a high-end summer camp for rich kids than a playground for the BM elite willing to foot the nearly twenty-thousand–dollar cost of the mediocre R.V.s they were flogging.

I had a tent, with its inflatable bed, single sheet, pillow, and burlap blanket that seemed pretty far from the 'glamping' that was advertised. Still, it was night, I was tired, and a bed, some food, and a shower were all I wanted. Strangely, both the toilets and showers were locked (early arrival work crew not being considered worthy of such niceties, these were being saved for 'full paying' camp members). I had a friend with an RV, and we were told tent people use RV facilities. I wondered then how non-RV people felt about that, but in the desert, one must survive, and finding a place to shit and wash wasn't going to be even a contender in needs for the survival game out there on the Playa.

It was a seven-hour line up just to get into the emerging Black Rock City. We had come almost a week early to work on set up—on top of that, a four-hour drive from Reno and half the previous day on a flight from Vancouver had me as dazed and confused as a newbie burner could be. But I was in the United States at Burning Man. Amazing! A dream comes true. I had a dream for over twenty years of going to this Playa ritual and celebration, never once believing it would be possible in my lifetime. Snapped up in the early days of pot-prohibition, I had been churned through the soul-grinding machinery of the U.S. penal system, barely survived in what my lawyer described as 'Gladiator School' and, after release, as a final punishment, banned for twenty years from returning. Nowadays, it sounds like a draconian punishment for possession of a plant; back then, lives were being destroyed daily for this substance that you can now get in fifty different flavours at your local dispensary. The irony was not lost on me as I picked up my legally obtained recreational bag of killer buds from a store, minutes from the airport in Nevada. The same bag would have got me one-to-three years on my previous visit, twenty-three years earlier.

Finally, I was home, in the desert, with my people. Twenty-three years since my last time in this country and one month since I was granted a waiver and my travel ban lifted. Back in the desert, doubled in age and searching for a way to release the trauma, guilt, and nightmares that still plagued me from my previous (hard) time here. Right now, it was 6:00 a.m., and all I wanted was rest.

By 9:30 a.m. I was noticeably hot in my tent but managed to fall asleep once more only to come to, ninety minutes later, when the tent hit one hundred degrees inside, despite the feeble attempt of the portable A/C to reverse the heat storm building in the tipi-like structure. Without shade over them, these tents would be unusable by 10:30 a.m. on any given day as hot as this first one (there was no forecast for anything but more heat). There was no option but to suit up and get out to begin building a pyramid that, to this point, I had only imagined.

What few painkillers I had left, I cherished like gold bars. Assorted spinal injuries and other sports and survival-related pain had me knowing, all too soon, that these would run out. Having lost my herbal pain remedy on the drive in (the only thing lost and arguably the most important), I was about to start construction of a seven-storey scale model of the Great Pyramid of Giza in one of the hottest Burning Man festivals on record, while detoxing a year's worth of medium-level painkiller use, and ultimate abuse.

Not something I looked forward to, but, I figured, nothing I couldn't handle. It was my first Burn, but far from my first rodeo. However, it might as well have been my first trip outside the house for all I knew about what was really about to happen. I know now it was 'nothing I couldn't handle', but that's only because, when push comes to shove, I will walk all the way to hell and back on my own.

This experience was to push me deeper into suffering and surrender than I had ever known. Burning Man is something different to everyone; it is said to give you what you need more than what you want. I needed saving, suffering, and if I could survive, salvation. Radical ritual was the theme this year, and my ceremony was about to begin—it was already feeling more like an exorcism.

No stranger to hard times (and hard time), I had been driven to the edge of my sanity on more than one occasion (some might argue that I crossed that line years ago), but hefting fifteen tons of steel up seven storeys and assembling it in a self-supporting pyramid, with nuts, bolts, ten-pound hammers, and power drills while hanging tethered high in the sky above the Nevada desert playa in the days leading up to the world-famous Burning Man festival, was to prove as monumental a feat for me, both physically and spiritually, as I had ever known.

Wrapped in winter-like clothes, with scarves, gloves, and goggles for the fast-moving dust, was essential. Any part of my pasty-white skin exposed to this desert heat, 70 SPF or not, would be cooked like bacon inside of an hour after 11:00 a.m. I've never been a sun baby—worshipping the sun from shaded and often air-conditioned arenas is something I'm known for. All my houses on my home island of Bali have been called igloos, which gives an idea of my comfort zone. I was so far out of my comfort zone on the Playa, starting with the oily sweat, acid reflux, and irritability of an unplanned detox—rehab in a pyramid-shaped cauldron fifty feet above ground at one hundred and five degrees in the shade—what could go wrong?

Comedowns from painkillers, for anyone who doesn't know, starts with annoying aches and pains, and on-and-off hot and cold sweats, and, depending on usage and type, can get worse in unimaginable magnitudes. On one end of the scale, there is the *Farewell My Concubine* style meltdown, where a junky will smash up everything in a house while vomiting, screaming, and praying for death, and, on the other, a bored housewife becoming grumpy and unapproachable because her Vicodin prescription ran out. I was somewhere in the middle.

By day two, withdrawal was in full swing. I knew the feeling from experience with harder stuff when I was much younger. I used to say, 'I've only done heroin once, for two years'. It was the same feeling this time, and I was shocked.

The modern painkiller never seemed to make me feel good enough to be deserving of a comedown that hinted of the sinister touch of smack. Still, it's all the same stuff dressed differently, and, in many situations, handed out by doctors like breath mints. Perfect white pills just seemed to soften the edges of life, pep you up a little as they calmed the nerves. My partner took them to make her life just a little more bearable and dull the aching truths she held in her heart. If I am honest, I took them because, knowing the pain she had and not being able to take it away, hurt me so bad that I followed her (willingly) down the road of softening the edges and making it all a little less scary. Her pain hurt me less if I was always a little high (and I have never had any issues with being a little high); now I had the added excuse of old injuries to medically justify my need. She and I were two beautiful souls, dulled in the areas that hurt most, but at least, with each other, able to light up in love and kindness.

That's how it felt as long as I stayed high, but now I was in the desert, alone in a hot sweaty tent or being lifted by a ten-storey cherry picker, higher and higher, in the driving desert sun as we pounded, bolted, spiked, and levered fifteen tons of metal piping into a pyramid-shaped, to-scale model of the Great Pyramid of Giza.

I had no idea why I was doing this (I still have never had it explained). In awe, I was watching all of Black Rock City being built around me, and I was sweating and hurting with the rank intensity of being tarred in the noonday desert sun, with no fucking feathers. This was purgatory, and I had paid to be here!

At night, or as soon as evening came and my tent dropped below ninety-seven degrees, I crawled into it for as many hours of lucid nightmares and screaming muscle spasms as I could fit into the hours before daylight. I never imagined these innocuous, polite-looking white pills would have a comedown as bad as anything I had ever felt. The dreams were all the same. I was making love with every partner I had ever had, and at the final moment before climax, they would turn into winged demons, drop me from their hook-like talons into a fiery pit below, and float above me while renouncing having ever loved me. They laugh as I writhed and burned and tried to push my organs back into the holes they were leaking from amidst a black tar-like substance which, at some point, I realised must have been my own blood.

When first light broke through my tent, at about 7:00 a.m., I would get up, wash with a handful of Wet Wipes, clean the sticky ooze masquerading as sweat from as much of me as possible, drink three litres of water, get dressed and go out to either stack bundles of pipes, weighing easily one hundred pounds each, or get out on the scaffolding like a Bedouin warrior with my tools and, eventually, a harness in case a gust of wind or missed step sent me actually falling into the burning eternal damnation of my morphine-deprived dreams. It was trading one pain for another. Strangely, the only antidote for losing my mind (in my tent that I had at that moment), to get over the suffering of killing my pain, was pain; it became the only panacea. If I found exhaustion, I found some measure of salvation. 'The saint and the thief are equal in exhaustion'. I had become one and the other by stealing part of my own soul in a quest for comfort and to placate my troubled heart. Burning Man would either cleanse me or kill me, and still now, I think it may have done both. 'What doesn't kill me makes me stranger'.

SAMUDAYA *(The Truth of the Cause of Suffering)*

It would be easy to blame any number of things for the consequences of the situation in which I found myself, dead centre. I could blame the camp for poor living conditions, dangerous work conditions, improper cooling, and lack of shade structure, but our camp was nicer than many, and becoming more beautiful by the day. I could say it was like the woman I loved, and the heartbreak she brought me on occasion, but I would also have to say she brought me more happiness than any partner I have ever had. I would realise, early in the experience, my heart was not broken but infinitely expanded from loving her, unrequited or not. There was a sense of balance in the unbalance of my life, and, once again, I was facing dualities—for each action a reaction and most importantly a lesson. I could blame the drug seeping from my body and shutting down key pleasure centres on its way out. Its insidious nature, like some biblical demon disguised as a best friend, custom tooled by master alchemists to grip the soul in such a way it never feels to be constricted until one tries to make it let go. However, this would be like the egg blaming the chicken.

I thought I knew the consequences and had prepared an antidote to make it all easier, but the Playa did not want to play with me that way. The antidote had been lost on the way in, which was divine surrender in play. I had never 'lost' medications in my lifetime, not until I was here in one of the harshest environments on Earth, doing the hardest work of my life. I was not meant to forget this experience. Hence I write these stories for myself as much as anyone. A man walks into the desert to burn for reasons sometimes only his heart knows. His head tries to deny them and search for solutions, but if the heart has purpose, the head will eventually concede.

Surrender—I had come there to detox far more than this one chemical; I had come to burn out twenty-five years of emotional baggage and spiritually stunting fears. There was to be no 'easy way'; I was there to burn like so many others, and burn I would. I had walked onto the face of the sun and chosen hard labour and painful contemplation to rip wide my slumbering body and expose the true light within me. I saw I had to divest the cravings and desires not acting in my own true satisfaction in life but taking me farther from it, even if doing so in a haze of narco half awareness. It was a type of spiritual surgery, done in the dust, on the edge of a pyramid, with no anaesthetic and what felt like a real possibility of catastrophic failure. At that moment, I thought all of it was only going to be pain and suffering, but, as they say, 'Once you've gone through hell . . . keep going'. There is no eject button at Burning Man. Getting out would have been more of an ordeal, and more painful than staying, and the one thing I had was the support of almost every person there.

Burning Man is an exercise in utopia, what perfection could look like if kindness was always everyone's default choice. That, or it, was a new type of hell/heaven scenario never imagined before, where you had to suffer every day to enjoy every night, and, at least for me, it depended on which side of a sweltering hot tent I was in. Paradise was never more than ten hours away or ten hours from ending. The twilight hours of sunset and sunrise allowed me to keep pushing towards true bliss. I had become too attached to paradise, needed to surrender to purgatory, find a way to move there like the man I once was, like the adaptive animals we are all born, and are slowly conditioned away from. There was no blame, no cause or root of my suffering, there was only surrender. I had to try and adapt to it …

NIRODHA (*The Truth of Cessation of Suffering*)

On day five, things started to ease; my tent was no cooler, nor was the sun less hot, but my soul was burning less, my suffering replaced with the pain of hard work, the pattern of repetition not for its own sake or to earn a dollar but to be part of something bigger than any of us. I still had no idea why I was building this monolithic structure, nor really even who I was building it for. That I was a second-class citizen of this plug-and-play utopia no longer mattered as the pipes rose higher and higher, and we began to see the possibility of a seven-storey pyramid emerging. The energy was galvanizing, and the excitement palpable. It was bigger than me, bigger than us, and we would see it finished or die trying.

It was then that she walked in. I think we recognised each other from first glance, but the introduction came slowly, and on my part with unusual hesitation. She, however, attacked life all around her, letting her voice, her opinion, her choices, and her presence be known wherever she moved. She was the energy I was lacking and the understanding I needed. We began to tell our stories, and the day turned into night as I slipped into her aspect and her eyes. This experience which had, until this point, been a biblical-scale punishment to me, with the emergence of this angelic woman, nothing changed other than I began to look forward to the next minute. I had hoped that someone here was as insane as me (which is to say, perfectly sane). In her words, I heard lessons, and in my state, where all of life had become ritual, I listened and obeyed.

I went out that night, just as she advised. Five days of metal, sweat, pain, and exhaustion, five days of questioning every moment and looking in each direction for a quick way out, I would finally shed my internal chains and march from the pyramid into the open desert as my people had over two thousand years ago. I heard my deceased grandfather from the grave say, 'It's about time; Jewish kids are not supposed to build pyramids in the desert'—bless him, he was a son of Zion and there was truth to his imagined words. What I went out to that night was just as amazing as parting the sea. It was the mobile, electro-centric, souped-up sound systems of Playa chaos spiralling in all directions like a fast-moving fractal. All I could be sure of was which way was up and that, often, only by falling to my knees. I saw such beauty as to make angels weep, and with them, I cried in joy, in pain, and in celebration for my life up until that moment, and the life I knew I would emerge into on the other side.

Unimaginable vehicles rolled by at a snail's pace, blaring music from another world; art for the sake of art crisscrossed the dark playa with thousands of neon-lit bikes; people scurried from all directions just to behold, to dance, to cry and laugh and love and give, and not a piece of garbage visible anywhere. People, at their best, humanity at its finest, art as a god, light as the foundation, and sound the unifying singularity that for those perfect seconds brought us all together in love and kindness. Utopia, indeed, and there I sat in front of a lone statue of Shiva silently unassuming amidst the chaos and cacophony of super-high-volume sound. Unconsciously, I was praying to all my friends, past, present, and future, lighting up that place where my love for each of them sits and telling them I am okay, they will be okay, and we will all survive if we never forget to love one another and love our beautiful desert, our beautiful planet, the beautiful home we all share. It was a come-to-Jesus moment—then I broke open completely. The passion and the beauty and the worship of something divine I had long ago dismantled re-emerged and lifted me, energised me, and downloaded a thousand forgotten dreams born in the dust and carried into life.

Each of us on that Playa was burning with our compassion, each replacing self with the tribe, and in caring for others and ourselves, we were being set free from the World Wide Web of misinformation. Unplugged, we were listening to our hearts, not our smartphones, and it was a symphony of information and delight only seen in children and the eyes of true genius. I had walked through hell, and now was the time to keep on walking. This was rapture, and, for this night at least, the end of suffering and start of salvation. How great a difference a day can make. Heaven had come to Earth and made of Earth my heaven.

MAGGA (*The Truth of the Path Leading to the Cessation of Suffering*)

Truth only works for most if they lie a lot of the time. Truth is relative and distorted and open to interpretation, but if you can challenge yourself to adhere to several well thought out concepts or 'states of being', then you are far more likely to live as close to real 'truth' as a human being can. We are flawed, and we make promises we can't keep, and act in the pursuit of money, pleasure, and ego. Some of us steal, almost all of us lie, and there are many amongst us who are downright unkind, and some straight-up calculatingly evil. These roles will always be filled until mankind ascends and the ego becomes an outdated construct (don't hold your breath for this one!).

We are all beautiful at our essence; our core essential construct is beautiful children of divine creation. We are born this way, and most die this way, and during this brief "intermission" called life, we attach all these egos and issues, heartaches and habits, kinks and cracks in the armour protecting us. We attach them onto our unchanged essence. We attach all our stresses, fears, and hopes onto our ever-unchanging principal architecture.

Our inner child, our little god and goddess, have once known the feeling of being idolised for our purity. As we grow and leave that awareness behind, we remain the same perfect being at our core. It never changes, and if we only allow ourselves, we can reconnect to it anytime we want. If we become aware of our fear and stress, we can relinquish them in just the same way, just as quickly and without so much as looking back. Just choose to stop. Stop everything. Stop being lonely. Stop not loving yourself. You are perfect; your essence is as beautiful and as pure as the day you were born. All these other things—loneliness, heartbreak, fear, and sorrow—just put them down and realise how beautiful you are. Know you are loved, that the world has beauty, and you are invited to share in it all. You deserve happiness as much as anyone; start acting in ways that make you happy. It's way easier than making yourself unhappy.

This is a download from Zion, direct from the mainframe, and open to whatever interpretation helps you sleep at night. It was shared with me at the precipice of what I thought I was strong enough to handle. I have been instructed to share it with you. Forgive everything, love everyone, choose kindness but not blindness. You know who your family is, and you know you are loved. Take care of your family, take care of yourself. Live a beautiful life to allow this to happen.

There is no instruction manual, but if you choose love over hate, kindness over cruelness, and generosity over hoarding, you are on the right path. Speak well of other people or not at all (unless there is information that can help your family; we are still about survival).

Choose honey in the heart, not evil, and try to earn and spend conscious of any pain your dollars might be causing. Cherish the beautiful moments, and try more and more to live only beautiful moments, and always, always extend a helping hand to a true soul in need.

Photo: **The Pyramid** - *Burning Man, 2017*

Polish Your Joy

Polish Your Joy!
Is strength the absence
of fear . . .
or acceptance?

Is courage
the absence of tears,
or the knowledge that they are rinsing
our soul before the storm?

Hiding emotions is a trick,
not a power.
Finding where they are hidden
is the science of empathy.

Own your fear and it will never own you.
Cherish your tears;
they are a connection
to the child in all of us,
they wash away pain.
They polish your JOY!

Photo: *Taro's joy* …
Credit: Fiorenzo Nisi.

Dying

As we sit resplendent
while all around us good men die,
though the light in our own eyes
will not extinguish
the pain that ever dampens that flame.

How like angry apes we must appear,
crying diamonds into caviar,
'Life is not fair'.

I am ashamed, some days, of just living . . .
when I have tried so very hard not to,
while others, who spent life preciously,
did no harm,
no evil,
with only a reward of darkness.

What then is on the other side?
The only hope is that the righteous
enter first, maybe those left behind
are here because they deserve it . . .

Perhaps suffering is just human—
an Earth Garden of pleasure and pain.

I'll cry for those that cannot cry,
for those that won't, and those
who wish they had.
Perhaps I have been up too long,
perhaps the pain and the pills and the dreams
I am escaping from
have tainted this long darkness.
I cannot claim any of the ideas I pen,
but if I have written a few words in my book of redemption,
if I have made a ripple in a sea of greed,
or said a word to cause even one person to pause
before their next act of unkindness,
then the sleep lost, the dreams missed, and any love
I did not see is small price to pay.

I just have to keep reminding myself
of the man I would choose to be,
in a perfect world.

Eternum

In the silent place reserved for travelling inwards,
where the soft velvet touch of your lips
become clouds to bounce and roll through,
as a child might, if lost in heaven.

Wet and humid air hangs between us
on breaths I can no longer tell
which one is breathing . . .
There, at the gates of paradise,
there, two become one . . .
there, where time stills
to a slow molasses crawl,
then stops,
freezing into that moment, where reality and duality
intersect —
singular spirituality.

Souls halfway to heaven,
bodies rolling on the earth;
bliss washes through every impeccable cell.
We are flying.

Flying through the red, gold, and green
airs of our collective pasts.
What is astral travel
if not space travel?

You are like a fuel cell igniting
a great engine through time.

Where is it going?
Only goddesses can guess
where it has been
on the sacred earth
of you and I.
Multiplied a hundred times,
for a thousand reasons
all comes back to one.

Love in Eternum—
the eternal
One.
One love, two souls.

Photo: *Taro, with Agustina Ardie, in front of the Shark car at Rainforest Pavilion, Wonderfruit Festival 2019.*

Finale

Today is a good day.
Today is the first day
I have begun to understand what is happening to me.
With clarity for the first time in my life,
I can move forward with purpose, most assured.
Today is a day I will never forget.
I understand all the pain, all the suffering,
all the wandering around the planet
looking for myself.
Today, I feel found.
Today, I have found myself and realised
the essential beauty in all things.
Loveissent always,
all ways.

Photo: *Alexander, carrying "Ascension" by Ali Agus, with Penny and Saul*
Credit: Jen Li.

In January 2020, Taro Zion Joy drowned, by accident. He released his last breath in a quiet pool in Bali—yet his spirit remains in this book, in his friends, and perhaps in you, the reader . . .

From Brother to Brother

By Alexander Arbess-Joy

Why do you cry for me? I was no saint.
Many of you I hurt;
For this, I am sorry.
Pain is a side of love;
Love is the reason we are here.
The pathway to love is not what you think, nor what you have been told.
You can't try love; you can only experience it.
To hurt is to love.
I was only here for a while—
more of an experiment to see if I could be mastered by love again;
that is why I tested your love,
because if you could love me, you could love anyone—
and that is what love is.

Even in my passing, I test you;
you should be furious with me;
I did a stupid thing,
but all you have is love and hurt; you impress me so.
If there is something I can teach, it is this:
die with love in your hearts, in total appreciation of all life, death, horror,
maiden, maniac, and king,
every bird, shepherd, lion, tiger, and twig.
Be so filled with love it emanates from your being in every interaction.
Dying like this means you lived like this—
there is nothing more to learn.

Photo: *Alexander and Taro*

KNOW I AM WATCHING OVER YOU ALL ON PLANET EARTH...

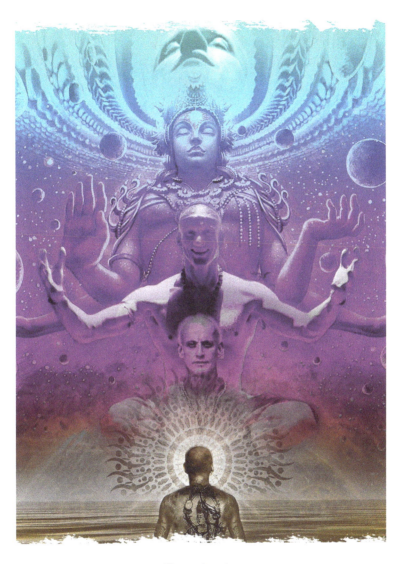

Photo: *Ascension*
Credit: Ali Agus

KNOW THERE WILL BE A NEW LIFE AND A NEW EARTH - I WILL BE THERE . . .

About the Book

Compiled by his family after his passing, this deeply emotional book honours Taro's memory and the legacy of his journey through life. International D.J., adventurous risk taker, soul-searcher, Taro Joy lived a life few of us can even imagine - including his demons! The *Tao of Taro* uses raw poetry, prose and significant photos to tell stories about his travels through the music industry, Tokyo's underworld, the U.S. prison system and spiritual revelations he had after several death defying experiences. These stories are of a boy's and a man's search for balance in chaos, which led him, towards the end of his life, to understanding. As a line from the book says, "Even the bad stuff is inspirational."

Acknowledgements

Sam Findley began this book with Taro in Bali in 2018. After Taro died his family, Penny Joy, Alexander Arbess-Joy, Jen Li and Saul Arbess nurtured it into this form in 2022. They recognize with deep appreciation the contributions of others on the journey. A beautiful book cover design "One Wave For The Storm Moon" by Miles Lowry, "Ascension" illustration by Ali Agus and the "Kannon" tattoo on Taro's back by Clay Decker. In addition, photos by Fiorenzo Nisi, Natalia Mansurova, Florian Siempelkamp, Alexander Arbess-Joy, Jen Li and others. Gratitude for loving support from Augustina Ardie, Ann Mortifee, Pauline Kelly and the many friends and supporters who, over the years, and from around the world, supported Taro's life and work – you know who you are!

Alexa, Taro's beloved daughter, was a critical part of his life and creative inspiration. With undying appreciation, we acknowledge her mom, Dita and stepdad, John La Mattery for their continued love, nurture and support. May she creatively blossom throughout her life and carry further the expansive joy, love and adventurous spirit of her father, Taro Zion Joy.

About the Author

Taro Zion Joy was born in York, England in 1971. From his earliest days he spent much of his life travelling. From teen years onward he embarked on many wild adventures and chronicled them in poetry and prose. Since his death, his work has been collected and compiled by his mother, Penny Joy, and his brother Alexander Arbess-Joy.

Taro began writing after having little academic success. Identified as dyslexic and told he would be unlikely to be capable of writing well, he became determined to change this prediction. He charted his own unique path and his exuberant creative spirit expanded in both life adventures, explorations and in recording many of the riveting stories of his several careers and passions. These included becoming a martial artist, an art gallery owner, an international DJ, affording extensive travel experience, briefly a prison inmate, and always a deep spiritual seeker who challenged every boundary he encountered.

Taro left this life, in Bali, in 2020. He is survived by his lovely daughter, Alexa and her mother, Dita. In addition by his own mother, Penny, her husband Saul, Taro's chosen father, his brother Alexander and wife Jen Li … as well as many lovers, friends and collaborators from around the world.

A year after his passing, the music track 'Trust the Molecules' was released. Taro's brother, Alex Joy and his wife Jen Li teamed with award winning record producer Neil McLellan of Prodigy fame to produce the single which featured voice recording by Taro and his mother Penny. We all felt Taro in the room when producing the track. Listen and download 'Trust the Molecules' here:

www.taooftaro.com

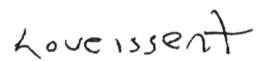

CPSIA information can be obtained
at www.ICGtesting.com
Printed in the USA
LVHW070412240423
744735LV00004B/6